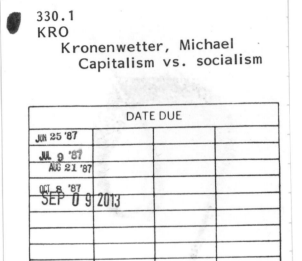

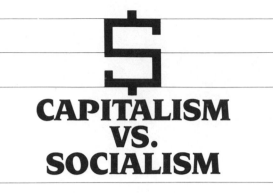

# CAPITALISM
## VS.
# SOCIALISM

# ECONOMIC POLICIES OF THE USA AND THE USSR

# CAPITALISM VS. SOCIALISM

BY MICHAEL KRONENWETTER

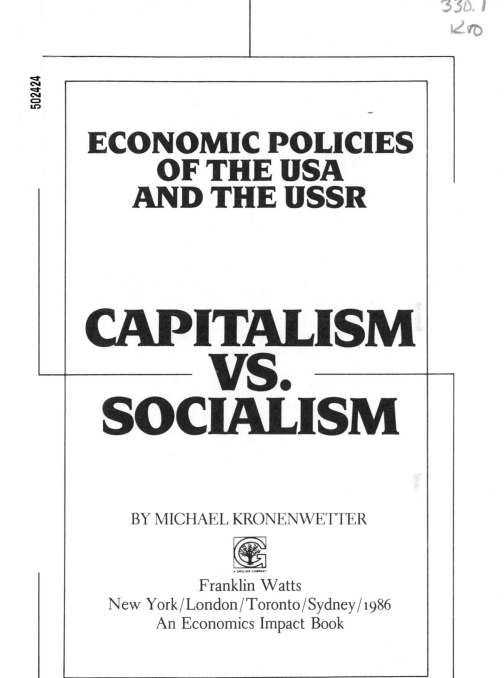

Franklin Watts
New York/London/Toronto/Sydney/1986
An Economics Impact Book

Photographs courtesy of:
The Bettmann Archive: pp. 7, 14, 28, 48;
Library of Congress: pp. 19, 39;
UPI/Bettmann Newsphotos: pp. 63, 66, 88;
Sovfoto: pp. 84, 95.

Library of Congress Cataloging in Publication Data

Kronenwetter, Michael.
Capitalism vs. socialism.

(An Economics impact book)
Bibliography: p.
Includes index.
Summary: Discusses the history of capitalism and
socialism, focusing on how these economic systems
function in the United States and the Soviet Union
today.
1. Comparative economics. 2. Capitalism—History.
3. Socialism—History. 4. United States—Economic
policy. 5. Soviet Union—Economic policy.
[1. Capitalism—History. 2. Socialism—History]
I. Title. II. Title: Capitalism versus socialism.
III. Series.
HB90.K76 1986          330.1          85-22579
ISBN 0-531-10152-5

# CONTENTS

# CAPITALISM
## VS.
# SOCIALISM

# INTRODUCTION:
# THREE QUESTIONS

## WHAT IS
## AN ECONOMIC SYSTEM?

Every society has a wide range of economic wants—needs and desires for goods and services. These economic wants are virtually unlimited, but the resources available to fulfill them are limited. A problem of every society, then, is this: how can its economy best be organized to fulfill unlimited wants from limited resources?

This broad question can be broken down into three others: What goods and services should the society produce? How should they be produced? For whom should they be produced (who should receive them)? The way in which a society answers these questions constitutes its economic system.

## HOW DOES
## A SOCIETY CHOOSE ITS
## ECONOMIC SYSTEM?

Generally speaking, a society chooses its economic system on the basis of three factors: tradition, ideology, and pragmatism. Tradition is the way in which things have been done before. Ideology has to do with the values of the society, what people believe is right and proper. Pragmatism is the effort to be practical, to find solutions that will work.

In any given society, at any given time, one or another of these factors may be dominant. Immediately after a revolution, for example, ideology may be considered overwhelmingly important. In the midst of a devastating economic crisis, pragmatism—the effort to find some way out of the crisis, whatever it may be—will probably take precedence. But over time, all three factors will play major parts in forming any nation's economic system.

## HOW ARE ECONOMIC SYSTEMS DEFINED?

There are a number of ways to describe economic systems. In this book, we will deal with them mainly in terms of the two dominant economic ideologies of our time, capitalism and socialism. These are the terms most commonly used by politicians, and by most other people, when discussing the major economic systems in the world today. They are not, however, the terms all economists prefer to use. For economists, the terms capitalism and socialism are not objective. They are too emotionally loaded, too politically ideological. Economists prefer to define economic systems as traditional, command, market, or mixed.

In a *traditional economy* economic decisions are made largely on the basis of the way they have been made in the past. Most primitive societies have traditional economies, in which people continue to organize their economic affairs in the same way as earlier generations.

In a *command economy* economic decisions are centralized. That is, they are made by a central authority—perhaps a dictator, or a government board. The people of the society are forced to carry them out whether they want to or not.

In a *market economy* economic decisions are decentralized. Citizens are left alone to make their own economic decisions. Rather than being directed (or dictated) from above, the course of the economy is determined by the total of all the private economic choices made by individuals acting on the basis of their own needs, desires, and inclinations.

A *mixed economy* combines features of two or more of the other types of economies.

In the modern world, traditional economies are rare. Economic conditions have changed so much in the past century that traditional economies simply cannot function efficiently today. Capitalist economic systems are primarily market economies, in which economic decisions are left up to private individuals. Socialist economies are forms of command economies, in which a central authority makes most of the important economic decisions. Most economics in the world today are, to some extent at least, mixed economies.

# 1

# THE FORERUNNERS OF CAPITALISM

The marketplace—on which capitalist societies depend for the answers to their economic questions—is not new. Nor are most of the practices which are today described as capitalistic. The ancient Egyptians engaged in many such practices, as did the citizens of the city-states of ancient Greece and of the Roman Empire. So did the merchants and traders of many African and Asian societies that existed long before most of Europe was "civilized."

But capitalism as we know it today is largely the result of developments that took place in the economies of Europe (including the British Isles) during that continent's passage out of the Middle Ages and into the modern era, a passage which took several centuries to complete.

## MANORIAL FEUDALISM

For roughly 800 years—from the ninth to the seventeenth centuries A.D.—the economies of Europe were dominated by the interrelated systems of feudalism and manorialism. While the two are closely related to each other, distinctions can be made between them. *Feudal ism* usually refers to the system of political and military arrangements by which Europe was organized during that time. *Manorialism* refers primarily to the society's economic arrangements. The specifics of those arrangements, both economic and political, varied from country to country and from century to century. The two systems were so intertwined, and the variations were so slight, that for the sake of simplicity, we will ignore those distinctions and speak of one system which we will call *manorial feudalism*.

The economy of medieval Europe was based on agriculture. Most of the people lived on and worked the land, and the main product produced by the economy was food. Because of this, the main source and symbol of wealth was land. But land meant much more than just economic wealth. Social prestige and political power also went with the land. Land, wealth, and power were divided up among the members of a relatively small class of people known as the nobility.

A map of a medieval kingdom that showed the lands controlled by the various nobles would be a fairly reliable guide to the wealth and power of those nobles as well. In theory at least, the entire kingdom would be under the control of the monarch, usually a king. He would keep several areas, and several castles, for himself. The rest he would divide, giving portions to his most important nobles. They, in turn, would keep some lands and towns for themselves and distribute the rest among lesser

*Peasants work on a plot in the shadow of the feudal castle.*

nobles. These would do the same, until the entire kingdom had been divided into ever smaller pieces of land, each under the authority of a noble. The larger pieces, and the more fertile lands, would be those of the most important nobles. The smaller portions of inferior lands would belong to the least important members of the nobility. These geographical units, with the houses and towns that went with them, were called *manors*.

Each of the nobles owed allegiance to the noble from whom he (or his ancestor) received his manor, and to the king from whom all power in the kingdom was passed down. This entire manorial structure was held together by bonds of political loyalty and financial responsibility. Each noble had obligations to those above and below him on the scale of wealth and power. A lesser noble was obliged to help his lord (the noble above him) in time of war, and was expected to give his lord a certain amount of the crops or other wealth his manor produced. The greater nobles were obliged to offer those below them help and protection in various circumstances.

The nobles did not work the land themselves. Instead, they relied on a much larger class of peasants to do that for them. The peasants had virtually no wealth or power. In return for their work on their lord's lands (and, in the case of the males, in return for their service in his wars), they received their lord's protection and the right to live on his lands.

Under this system, the concept of ownership had little meaning. People, nobles, and peasants alike "held" their lands and the right to use them more than they "owned" them. Their rights were usually passed down from one generation to another. This was even true of many peasants; while they owned no land at all, they inherited from their fathers the right to live on and work a given piece of land on the lord's estate. The rights of both nobles and peasants were protected by law and tradition.

Many of the larger manors contained within their borders some manufacturing industries. These were small shops, worked by a single blacksmith or weaver, or a single family skilled in a trade. The lord of the manor would receive a portion of the products that were produced on his manor. If more of a product was produced than could be used within the manor, it would be sold.

As an economic system, manorial feudalism was both simple and nondynamic. It was, in other words, traditional. It carried on with relatively little change from century to century, producing very little in the way of economic or technological progress. The excess wealth that was produced tended to get used up in economically unproductive activities—mainly the seemingly endless succession of wars, small and large, that were a constant feature of medieval life.

But then, on August 3, 1492, Christopher Columbus sailed west from Spain in an attempt to find a western route to India, and the economy of Europe—after centuries of remaining virtually unchanged—began a great transformation.

## MERCANTILISM

Actually, it would be many decades before the discovery of the Americas would have its great impact on Europe's economy. But when it came, it would be enormous. Even before Columbus's voyage, political changes in Europe were making economic change necessary. A variety of wars had the double effect of making the kings more powerful and teaching them the value of money.

For centuries, Europe had been a patchwork of shifting alliances between kings and nobles. By the fifteenth and sixteenth centuries, however, it was settling into a pattern of recognizable, newly emerging nation-states. These states, each with its own king, tended to be extremely competitive with each other, both commercially and militarily.

The two forms of competition were related. Raising and supplying armies on the scale required was expensive. This meant that the nations' economies had to produce a surplus over and above what was necessary to maintain a peaceful existence, a surplus which could be used to purchase the arms, horses, supplies, and mercenary soldiers needed to wage war. Because of this, the kings had to make their economies more productive.

In practice, this meant that less of the nation's economic activity could be devoted to agricultural products, which were used mostly at home, and more had to be devoted to the production of goods that could be traded abroad. The proceeds from that trade could be used to finance the king's wars. But in order for that to happen, there had to be what is called a *favorable balance of trade*. That is, the foreign trading had to be done so more wealth flowed into the country than out of it.

The kings did everything they could to assure this favorable balance of trade. They tried to promote the importation of resources from their own colonies, since those colonies required very little wealth in return. At the same time, they did what they could to discourage the importation of goods from competing nation-states. Those goods would have to be paid for, resulting in an outflow of wealth from the home country. While encouraging manufacturing industries within their own kingdoms to produce goods for sale abroad, they put tariffs, or special duties, on any goods imported from competing states.

All of these efforts were made for political as well as commercial reasons. They were made not only to promote the nations' own interests, but to do so at the expense of their rivals. To a great extent, that was the whole point. Trade and other forms of commerce were not purely financial activities. They were weapons in the great power struggle between nations.

This system—in which the nations of Europe competed with each other for commercial supremacy by encouraging the development of their own manufacturing industries while attempting to achieve a favorable balance of trade—was called *mercantilism*. Although many forms of the old system remained well into the eighteenth century, mercantilism eventually came to overshadow manorial feudalism as the dominant economic reality in Europe.

Mercantilist economies were primarily command rather than market systems. That is, the key economic decisions were made not by the demands of the marketplace, but by the mandates of the rulers. The monarchs and their financial advisers decided what had to be done and their orders were passed down to the merchants, shippers, bankers, and others who would have to carry them out. In this respect, mercantilism was the opposite of capitalism, which as we shall see is first and foremost a market system. And yet, in a number of ways, it was mercantilism that laid the foundation stones for capitalism's development.

## GOLD AND SILVER

One of the most important foundation stones was the growing importance of money—a medium of exchange that would be accepted by both buyers and sellers of goods. Money was not terribly important in traditional economies where most transactions were carried out by barter, the simple trade of one product or service for another. But in complex dealings barter was unsatisfactory. This was particularly true when it came to the complexities of foreign trade.

If a king wanted to buy horses, for example, and his wealth was in the form of a surplus production of cloth, he had to find someone with horses to trade who also wanted cloth. But what if he could not find such a person? What if the only merchant with horses to trade had no need for cloth? What if all he wanted was iron ore? Then the king had to find someone with iron ore to trade who did want his cloth. Then he could trade the cloth for the iron ore, after which he could turn around and trade the iron ore for the horses. But what if the merchant with the iron ore didn't want cloth either? What if he wanted tapestries, say? Or carrots?

Money made everything much simpler. If there was a medium of exchange accepted by all parties, then the king could sell his cloth to anyone who wanted it. He would receive money in exchange for the cloth, and he could use the money to buy horses from anyone who had them for sale. The horse-seller, in turn, could use the money to buy anything *he* wanted. Money was a virtual necessity for large-scale trade, and particularly for foreign trade which became increasingly important throughout the fifteenth and sixteenth centuries.

Money in those days meant primarily the metals gold and silver. They were durable, easily recognizable, and highly valued by people all over the known world. It was largely because of gold and silver that the discovery of the New World was so important to the kings of Europe.

It was seen as a rich source of the precious metals (as well as of other natural resources). Consequently, an important element of the mercantilist policies of the European monarchs was to encourage the colonization of the New World, grabbing great chunks of it (and the precious metals they assumed it contained) for themselves.

## THE CHARTERED COMPANY

Colonization and the increasing importance of foreign trade led to the development of another important foundation stone of capitalism, the *chartered company*, the forerunner of the modern capitalist corporation.

Foreign trade, which was the backbone of mercantilist policy, was expensive to carry out, requiring large amounts of money to finance trading expeditions to the far corners of the world. Since the monarchs were reluctant to use their own money (even when they had it), they adopted the practice of chartering companies to conduct the trade for them. That is, they licensed groups of individuals to trade in their nation's goods.

These companies were usually chartered to act in a specific region of the world. Each was given a monopoly to conduct a nation's trade with a particular area. England's Muscovy Company, for example, was given the right to carry out England's trade with Russia, while the Levant Company traded with the nations surrounding the eastern end of the Mediterranean Sea.

All the great mercantilist nations—England, France, Portugal, Spain, and Holland—chartered such companies. Many of them were authorized to do much more than trade. Some actually founded colonies and ran them. For example, it was through the British East India

Company that the small country of England came to control the huge nation of India in the seventeenth century (a control that lasted until the 1940s).

The activities of these companies were historically significant, but more important than their trading and colonizing activities was their organization of what were called *joint stock companies*.

In joint stock companies, merchants or others with surplus wealth (more than they needed to supply themselves with the necessities of life) would pool their wealth to finance a business venture. Each received stock in the company, which amounted to a share in the enterprise. This is similar to what investors in modern capitalist companies do today. In that way, the mercantilist joint stock company can be considered an early form of capitalism. What's more, the businessmen invested with the expectation that they would get more out of the venture than they put into it. That is, they risked their resources in the expectation of making a profit. Once again, they were acting like modern capitalists. As we shall see, the profit motive is at the center of the capitalist economic system.

Although in some ways the joint stock company can be seen as containing the seeds of the capitalist system that would eventually replace it, the joint stock company was in other ways very much a mercantilist institution. Its investors were acting in their own self-interest (that is, from capitalist motives) but the company itself had broader purposes than making a profit for its investors. And it owed its existence to those other purposes. The

*The Old East India Wharf
at London Bridge*

chartered company was expected to act on behalf of the nation that had granted its charter. It was not so much a private organization, working to promote the private welfare of its stockholders, as an arm of the state, chartered to carry out state policy.

Sometimes these interests—the private interests of the investors and the public interests of the state—came into conflict. In such cases, the company was required to act in the best interests of the state. At other times, there would be no clear conflict, but rather a confusion of interests. That confusion was an inevitable element of mercantilism. The system, by its nature, mixed patriotism and the profit motive together, just as it mixed political and economic policies, attempting to make economic activities a mere branch of political action.

Not everyone saw this confusion as either inevitable or desirable. At least one man saw it as destructive, and foresaw the death of mercantilism as a result of it. In the revolutionary year of 1776, in a book that was the first major document in the history of capitalism, *An Inquiry into the Nature and Causes of the Wealth of Nations*, Adam Smith set out his views on what should replace mercantilism.

# THE EMERGENCE
# OF CAPITALISM

The author of *An Inquiry into the Nature and Causes of the Wealth of Nations*, Adam Smith, was a Scottish economist and professor of moral philosophy. He was very much a man of the Enlightenment. Like other leaders of that philosophical movement, he tried to look at reality in a new way, to discover—through scientific observation and reasoning—the natural laws that governed it. What Newton did for physics, and Descartes did for mathematics, Smith attempted to do for economics. He set out to discard the old ideas of how economic activity *should* work. Instead, he wanted to discover the way it *did* work.

In *The Wealth of Nations*, he presented the results of his observations: a new and compelling vision of an economic landscape shaped by natural forces as strong and uncontrollable as the forces of wind and rain.

It would be hard to overestimate the significance of Smith's vision on western economic thought. His book has been called the single most important work on the subject of political economy, and the foundation upon which the study of classical economics was built. It was certainly the foundation upon which capitalism—sometimes called the free enterprise system —was built. Even today, more than two hundred years later, it remains the most widely quoted argument ever written in favor of the capitalist system.

## THE VISION OF
## ADAM SMITH

In *The Wealth of Nations*, Adam Smith explored many details of the economic landscape. But the bedrock on which the landscape rested was the question of wealth itself. What constituted wealth? Or, put another way, what was value? Goods are exchanged on the assumption that they have some value outside themselves, value that can be compared to the value of other goods, and therefore exchanged for them. But what is that value? Where does it come from?

Smith began his exploration of this question by making a distinction between a commodity's *value in use* (its usefulness) and its *value in exchange* (what it can be traded for). These two kinds of value, he pointed out, were very different things. To illustrate, he used the example of two commodities. One of them, water, was an enormously useful thing, a necessity, yet in most circumstances it would bring very little if anything in exchange. Diamonds, on the other hand, were virtually useless, yet they would bring a great deal in exchange.

As his subject was the wealth of nations, it was value in exchange and not value in use that most interested Smith. Having narrowed the question, he went on to

*Adam Smith, author of*
The Wealth of Nations

[18]

analyze the source of a commodity's value in exchange. This, he explained, was threefold. It comes first from the amount of land (or of other natural resources) needed to produce it; then from the amount of capital which has to be invested in the process; and, finally, from the amount of the labor of all kinds that goes into the commodity's production. According to Smith, the most important of the three—the main source of any commodity's value— is labor: the human energy, talents, and effort that have gone into its production.

The cost of each of these three factors can be measured. The cost of land is stated in rent, the cost of capital is measured in the interest that has to be paid on the investment, and the cost of labor appears in the wages of those who work to produce the commodity.

These three costs together add up to the "natural price" of the commodity. When the commodity is taken to the marketplace for sale, it should bring something close to that natural price in exchange—if there is a balance of supply and demand. In other words, if there is an approximate balance between the amount of the commodity offered for sale and the amount of the commodity for which there are willing buyers, the market price (what the commodity will actually bring in exchange) will be roughly equivalent to the natural price.

That rough balance between supply and demand does not always exist, however. When it does not, the actual market price of a commodity may be either more or less than its natural price. If the supply of the commodity is greater than the demand for it, the market price will be forced down below the natural price. Suppliers will lower their price in order to persuade the few available buyers to purchase from them and not from someone else. If, on the other hand, the demand is greater than the supply, and there are more eager buyers than there are units of the commodity available for sale, the market price will be driven higher than the natural price. This is because the many buyers will offer more for the commodity in order to persuade the relatively few sellers to sell to them rather than to someone else.

In either of these cases the market, left to its own devices, will begin to correct itself. If the supply is greater than the demand, producers will cut back on their production, eventually lowering the supply. This will increase demand relative to the supply and bring the market price back up toward the natural price. If the demand is greater than the supply, producers will increase their production in order to take advantage of the increased demand. This will increase the supply relative to the demand and bring the market price back down closer to the natural price.

The end result of the process is to assure that commodities will be available to consumers at something close to the natural price. This is desirable for all concerned, not just for the consumers. The natural price provides a fair share for everyone involved in the production of the commodity—laborers, investors, and renters alike—as well as a reasonable cost to the consumer.

A price much higher than the natural price might seem desirable for the producers, but it would be unfortunate for the consumer who would then have to pay more than the commodity's natural worth. At the same time, a price much lower than the natural price would be just as unfortunate, for both producers and consumers, because at such a low price the supply of the commodity would dry up. Producers would be unwilling to produce it because it would cost more to produce than it could be sold for. Under such circumstances, the commodity would cease to be available to consumers at all.

Of all the elements of the process, the welfare of the consumer most interested Smith. He wrote: "Consumption is the sole end and purpose of production." He went even further, stating that "the interest of the producer ought to be attended to only so far as it may be necessary for promoting that of the consumer."

## THE INVISIBLE HAND

The two main features of Smith's economic landscape are self-interest and economic freedom. These two essential elements balance and complement each other. Self-interest, according to Smith, is the great motive force of all economic activity. Economic freedom is the mechanism that allows that force to accomplish its goals.

As Smith explained the process in *The Wealth of Nations*, the main reason that people engage in economic activity is self-interest. This is as true of investors as it is of manual laborers, and as true of candle makers as it is of bankers. People produce not in order to add to the general wealth of nations (or mankind) but to get something for themselves. People, Smith pointed out, get their bread not by appealing to the generosity of the baker, nor their meat by appealing to the fine feelings of the butcher. Instead, they appeal to the self-interest of those producers by giving them something (usually money) in return for their products.

The consumers, needing that food, must take part in some economic activity to get the money to exchange for it. Economic self-interest—the desire for gain—is the force that powers all economic activity.

In order for that activity to prosper, Smith argued, economic freedom is necessary. When individuals and business enterprises alike are allowed to compete and bargain freely, each fighting for its own private self-interest, the best possible economic results are obtained for the society as a whole. As we've already seen, such free competition in the marketplace tends to drive prices toward the natural price, but competition functions equally well in other areas of economic activity. Competition among manufacturers tends to produce better products. Competition among workers tends to produce more skill and harder work. And so on, throughout the range of economic activities.

Therefore, the less the government, or any other authority, interferes with the private economic competition of individuals, the better for everyone. The government, as Smith saw it, has three legitimate and necessary functions.

First, it has to protect the state against invasion by an outside power. Second, it has to protect the individuals within the society from unjust actions of their neighbors. Third, it has to build and maintain those public works and public services which are beyond the scope of private enterprise. With these exceptions, Smith believed that the government should keep out of the economic affairs of private citizens.

Even private citizens whose economic activities are protected by the state should themselves avoid, for the most part, acting from motives other than their own self-interest. Smith distrusted the economic activities of private individuals attempting to act for the public good almost as much as he distrusted those of the government. As he put it, "I have never known much good done by those who affected to trade for the public good. . . . By pursuing his own interest [the individual] frequently promotes that of the society more effectively than when he really intends to promote it."

Self-interest, then, is not just a necessary evil; it is, however unintentionally, a positive force for good. This is the heart of Smith's argument. The economy is such a vast and complicated thing that no individual, no group, and no government can understand it well enough to control its functioning. It can only function well if all the forces of individual self-interest are allowed to compete with one another in the greatest possible economic freedom.

> All systems either of preference or of restraint, therefore, being thus completely taken away, the obvious and simple system of natural liberty establishes itself. . . . Every man, as long as he does not violate the laws of justice, is left perfectly free to pursue his own interest his own way.

Smith was calling for what has come to be known as *laissez-faire*. A French term, literally meaning "to let do," it is commonly used as a plea to government to allow people to handle their own economic affairs in their own way. Smith believed that allowing this would result in benefits not just for individuals pursuing their own self-interest but for the society as a whole. As Smith explained the process in one of the most famous passages in *The Wealth of Nations:* "He intends only his own gain, and he is in this, as in many other cases, led by an invisible hand to promote an end which was no part of his intention." That is, the good of society.

Ever since 1776, many supporters of capitalism continue to praise Smith's "invisible hand" as the system's major justification and defense against its critics. The alternative to a free enterprise system, they argue, is a command economy, in which economic decisions are made by the government. And no government, no individual or group of individuals—however well intentioned—can ever direct an entire economy as wisely and benevolently as the "invisible hand."

## THE DIVISION
## OF LABOR

Another feature of Smith's economic landscape that would play an important part in the understanding of capitalism was his concept of the division of labor.

It was the division of labor, Smith believed, that enabled people to move beyond the stage of individual subsistence into a stage of social organization in which surplus goods could be produced. It was the division of labor that made trade and commerce possible.

As early as tribal times, Smith explained, some individuals discovered that they were better at making certain things (weapons, say) than other members of the society were. When they were able to produce more of those things than they needed for their own use (a surplus), they found that they could barter that surplus for things that other members of the society were better at producing than they were.

Previously everyone, or at least every family unit, had had to produce everything they needed for themselves. They had to be entirely self-sufficient in all things, which left them little time or energy to become more productive. But this newly discovered ability to exchange their surplus production for the surplus production of others made it possible for individuals to concentrate their energies in specific occupations. Weavers made cloth, tanners made leather, masons worked with stone, and so on. Then they exchanged their surpluses with each other. This was a division of society's labor, and it benefited society as a whole. Since individuals could now spend their working hours at a single trade, they became better at it than they could have when they had to spread their time and efforts over a wide variety of tasks. As a result, more and better products became available to be distributed, by exchange, throughout the society.

With the growth of manufacturing industry, which was taking place in Europe in Smith's time, the importance and value of the division of labor was becoming ever more clear. Just as society's labor as a whole was divided by individuals entering specific trades, the specific labor of a given factory was divided among the departments and workers within it.

To make his point, Smith used what has become a famous example, that of a factory producing that most humble of products, the common pin. It would be hard to imagine a more simple object, and yet, as Smith pointed out, the manufacturing of a pin could be broken down into eighteen separate operations. One worker forms the wire, another cuts it, another whitens it, another sticks the completed pins into papers for handling and sale, and so forth. The benefit to society of the division of labor within a pin factory was the same as that of the division of labor within society as a whole: greater efficiency and improved product. Several people working according to the principle of division of labor could produce many times the number of pins in a day that the same people could produce if each did all eighteen tasks themselves.

A valuable offshoot of the division of labor was, according to Smith, the production of special labor-saving machinery which could, in its turn, greatly increase the efficiency of production of specific goods. Given the responsibility for a specific task, a worker tended to concentrate his or her efforts on finding easier methods of doing it (the invisible hand of self-interest once again). Consequently, the worker was liable to come up with some new labor-saving device to make the job easier. Smith maintained that this function of the division of labor accounted for the increase in labor-saving machinery which was even then providing the manufacturing industries of the western world a spur that contributed to the advent of the Industrial Revolution.

## REVOLUTION IN TECHNOLOGY

The Industrial Revolution was a vast and complicated process. It involved drastic economic, technological, social, and cultural changes, and it is impossible to say exactly when those changes began. In the broadest sense, it can be said that the Industrial Revolution began whenever and wherever the first manufacturing enterprise was mechanized. It is still going on, perhaps over a larger portion of the earth than ever before. And there is no end in sight.

Workshop of Boulton & Watt
for the manufacture of
steam engines in England

But in the sense in which the term is usually used, the Industrial Revolution started in the British textile industry in 1733, when a man named John Kay invented the "flying shuttle." This device greatly improved the efficiency of the weaving process, more than doubling the amount of cloth a single worker could produce. Increasing efficiency through the use of new machines was what the Industrial Revolution was all about.

Contrary to Adam Smith's theory, workers at first resisted the "flying shuttle," as they would resist many of the other new machines. But the Industrial Revolution swept forward. A series of new, more efficient inventions transformed the British textile industry, changing it from a collection of little factories into a modern industry in the three decades from 1760 to 1790.

Similar dramatic changes were taking place elsewhere in the British economy at the same time. Tools of almost every kind were being improved. The use of coal instead of wood to fuel factories was made possible by the invention (several decades before) of Thomas Newcomen's steam engine which pumped water out of the coal mines, making them both safer and more efficient. But it was the more advanced steam engine invented by James Watt in the 1760s that provided the driving power for the Industrial Revolution. This new engine made it possible for steam-driven machines to be used almost anywhere. Mills, for example, no longer had to be built near waterfalls. They could be set up nearer the sources of raw materials, or of markets, greatly increasing efficiency.

By early in the nineteenth century, advances in manufacturing were matched by great advances in communications and transportation. The new steam engine made the railroads possible and, beginning in the 1820s, the iron tracks rapidly crisscrossed Europe. Robert Fulton's steamboat, which appeared in 1807, greatly improved the speed and reliability of ocean travel.

Although the Industrial Revolution began in England, it soon spread through Belgium, France, and Germany, and then crossed the ocean to the United States. America had already both affected and been affected by the Revolution. The great increase in production in the British textile industry, for example, had been made possible by the vast supply of American cotton; and the needed increase in that supply had been made possible by the invention of the cotton gin by the American Eli Whitney in 1793.

Whitney represented the Industrial Revolution in another way as well. In 1798, having failed to make his fortune from his cotton gin, he started a musket factory. Using the newest technology, he produced muskets with parts so standardized that they were actually interchangeable. This was something new in an age in which muskets had always been made by hand. Whitney's was the first musket factory in the United States to use the modern methods of mass production that made such standardization possible.

The Industrial Revolution was the result of many things, all which came together, first in England and Europe and then in the United States, in the eighteenth and nineteenth centuries. First was the expanded market for manufactured goods made possible by a dramatic increase in population throughout much of the western world. Second were the great technological advances that seemed to spring up like mushrooms after a rain, both in Europe and the United States. Third were the efficiencies of the division of labor which Adam Smith had explained in *The Wealth of Nations*. But the Industrial Revolution needed something else as well. It needed capital.

## THE NEW IMPORTANCE OF CAPITAL

The widespread and sudden industrialization required huge amounts of capital (money) to finance it. The new machinery was expensive, as were the factories needed to house it. Although individual wages were low, payrolls taken as a whole added up to substantial amounts of money. Time was needed to build the new factories and to begin production, and until the factories were producing, none of these enormous expenses could be paid for from income. They had to be paid for by investment, by capital.

The result of this requirement was to transform what had been essentially command, mercantilist economies into essentially market, capitalist economies. The major economic decisions, which had earlier been made by monarchs and their financial advisers, were now being made by businessmen—the individuals who put up the money for the new enterprises.

This was not an inevitable result. Industrialization does not, in and of itself, necessarily result in capitalism. A certain amount of industrialization had taken place under the mercantile system, and even before. The capital for it had been supplied by governments (out of taxes), or by joint stock companies or bankers, while the enterprises themselves remained under the authority of the governments. The future would prove that industrialization, even massive industrialization, can be carried out by socialist and even fascist economies. But for whatever reasons, the first century of the Industrial Revolution brought with it the development of the capitalist system. In other words, the relative role of capital in the economic process increased so much that it came to dominate it; and the providers of capital became the most influential figures in the entire process, and to control it.

For the most part, the providers of capital were private individuals. Some of them contributed their own money to finance new ventures, but some contributed mostly other people's money. They formed joint stock companies, or other investment pools, convincing as many people as possible to invest in them. Some of the investors contributed a great deal of money while others contributed quite small amounts. In theory, all the stockholders in such a company would be part owners of it, and would have a share in whatever endeavors the company might finance. When the investment company was honestly and competently run (as was often not the case) each of the individual investors would make a profit from their investment. In any case, each part owner would have a say in all the major decisions faced by the company.

In reality, the control and the power to make decisions rested with the relatively few capitalists who ran the companies, not with the more numerous investors whose money was being used. These skilled handlers of other people's money, then, were as powerful as those other early capitalists who supplied their own money to finance the giant enterprises that grew out of the Industrial Revolution. And their power easily overwhelmed the power—at least the effective power—of the entire labor force.

In many respects, their power rivaled even that of the governments in whose nations they functioned. For, to a surprising extent, the governments of the time practiced the *laissez-faire* policies which Adam Smith recommended. Particularly in the United States, there were few taxes on capital or on the profits made from capital. In most industries, there were virtually no governmental regulations.

Governments might still attempt to regulate trade (as opposed to production) by measures such as tariffs, but since such regulation tended to promote domestic industries rather than to harm them, they ultimately increased rather than diminished the power of those industries and the men who ran them. (They were virtually all men. Women of wealth were discouraged from entering business, as it was considered "unladylike." Women who had no wealth, on the other hand, were put to work in the new factories at the lowest possible wages.)

## BENEFITS

The combination of rapid technological advances with *laissez-faire* capitalism produced enormous benefits. It greatly increased what Adam Smith had written about, the wealth of the nations in which the Industrial Revolution took place.

Such familiar products as textiles and pottery were suddenly turned out in quantities that had been unimaginable only decades before. Not only were they more widely available, they were of better quality than ever before, and—thanks to the more efficient means of pro-

[33]

duction and the suddenly abundant supply—they could be had at cheaper prices.

Beyond that, a wide range of new products, from bicycles to precision tools, became available for the first time in history. Both the production and the consumption of goods soared throughout the industrialized countries.

The production of new and more plentiful products resulted in the search for new markets abroad as well as the search for the raw materials needed to feed the ever-growing industries. This, in turn, led to an increased emphasis on colonial and imperialistic ventures in the rest of the world. While this had its dark side, it was argued that it not only enriched the European nations but speeded up the economic and cultural development of the colonized nations as well.

The dawn of industrial capitalism was, it seemed clear to its supporters, an enormous success. It had increased everything: production, consumption, economic efficiency, the quality of manufactured goods. Overall, it had increased the total wealth of mankind by an unprecedented amount.

# THE RESPONSE OF SOCIALISM

The new economic system was not originally called "capitalism" by its supporters. That term was coined in the middle of the nineteenth century by its enemies, whose alternative to that system we will discuss in this chapter.

But before looking into that alternative, it is necessary to examine why the new system, with benefits so clear and so enormous, produced enemies at all. The reason was that those benefits, which seemed so obvious to the businessmen who profited from them, were not nearly so clear to the vast numbers of laborers who worked in their factories.

The new system, as we have seen, was built on the principle of competition for economic advantage. Not all that competition was between different businessmen, competing with each other to produce better products at better prices. There was also a very basic competition which ran through the entire economy. It was the competition for economic advantage between the businessmen on one hand and the workers they employed on the other.

Adam Smith had recognized that this competition—this conflict of self-interests—was central to industry. It was to the advantage of the employers to produce goods at the lowest possible cost of production. The difference between that cost and what they could sell the goods for was, after all, their profit. One of the major costs of production was labor, the wages paid to the workers who produced the goods. Clearly, it was in the employers' interest to keep the cost of that labor as low as possible. Equally clearly, it was in the interest of the workers to keep the cost of their labor (their wages) as high as possible.

There was then, inevitably, a conflict between the interests of what Smith referred to as the "masters" and the "workmen." And, in this conflict, Smith recognized, the "masters" had the advantage.

The reason for this advantage had to do with the ease with which the "masters" could work together. In order for either group to successfully compete with the other, it was necessary for the members of that group to combine, to join together in action for their mutual benefit. And, under the brand of capitalism which first grew up in England (and later in the United States) it was much easier for the "masters" to combine than it was for the "workmen." As Smith put it: "People of the same trade seldom meet together, even for merriment and diversion, but the conversation ends in a conspiracy against the public, or in some contrivance to raise prices. It is impossible indeed to prevent such meetings by any law which . . . would be consistent with liberty and justice." Consequently, no laws to prevent such combinations of *employers* existed. On the other hand, laws did exist which effectively prevented such combinations among their employees. Some of these laws had been established long before, under an entirely different economic system. Some were put through the Parliament by the growing influence of the wealthy new "masters," working together in precisely the kinds of combinations that the laws were designed to keep their "workmen" from forming. *Laissez-faire* tended, in actual practice, to be applied much more generously to the first group than to the second.

Even if these legal obstacles to forming combinations of "workmen" hadn't existed, the "masters" would have had a natural advantage. There were fewer of them. It is much easier for a small group of individuals to meet together, to recognize common interests and take common action, than for a large group to do the same.

As a result of these natural and legal advantages, the early capitalist businessmen profited immensely. They built great industries and amassed huge fortunes. The workers who provided the labor for those industries profited to a much smaller extent. Indeed, many of them suffered enormously.

## A WIDENING GULF

Working conditions in the factories of the Industrial Revolution were hard at best. At worst, they were horrible. The owners of the factories were intent on keeping their profits as high as possible. One way was to keep their workers' wages as low as possible. Another way was to work the laborers as long and as hard as they could. With virtually no restraints on their treatment of the workers, they managed to work them very long and hard indeed.

Most industrial workers of the mid- to late nineteenth century worked at least twelve hours a day. Many worked considerably longer. The average British textile worker, for example, spent thirteen and a half hours a day actually working. The employer allowed about one and a half hours of rest time each day, since it was discovered that with any less, the worker could not have continued to function adequately on the job. This meant a worker would have to spend a full fifteen hours of every workday in the factory. Simple arithmetic shows that this left only nine hours a day for sleep, family responsibilities, and all other activities. Leisure was unknown.

The standard work week in the factories was six days. In some industries, however, in order to have Sunday off the workers had to work all night on Saturday.

Just as there were no laws regulating the amount of time an employer could require workers to work, there were no laws to regulate conditions in the factory. These were often extremely unhealthy, and sometimes deadly. Accidents on the job were frequent, and often if a worker was injured so badly that he could not work, he was simply fired.

Work-related disease was even more common than accidents. For example, stone grinders, who spent their long workdays breathing in stone dust, were subject to a lung sickness called "grinder's disease." It has been reliably estimated that in Britain in the middle of the nineteenth century, fully half of all the stone grinders aged thirty and over had the disease. All of them over fifty had it.

Although the usual term for the workers in the factories was "workmen," many of them were women and children. In some industries, the majority of them were. This was only partly because there were many single women whose families could not support them, and

Men, women, and children of all ages
leaving a New England factory at the end
of a workday in mid-nineteenth century

many families headed by women whose husbands had deserted them or (more commonly) died. It was mostly because many men were unable to support their families by themselves, even working twelve to fifteen hours a day. At one point during this period, the average working class family in Britain was made up of one man, one woman, and three children. Of them, the man, the woman and one of the children worked.

If working was hard, not working was even worse. There was no unemployment insurance, and no welfare system until well into the nineteenth century. (Even when they came, the protections they provided were few and ineffectual.) Wages were so low that it was impossible for families to save against the disaster of unemployment. And unemployment was virtually inevitable. The surge in population that occurred around this time was matched by a surge in the technology and organization of agriculture as well as of industry. Advances in agricultural technology lowered the relative demand for agricultural labor. As a result, large numbers of rural people flocked to the cities to find work in the factories. They produced a huge supply of labor that often overwhelmed the demand for it. At the same time, demand for the products of the factories fluctuated. This not only kept wages low, it produced periodic layoffs. It was not uncommon for one-half to one-third of the workers in a given industry to be thrown out of work. And, in those times, being thrown out of work meant being thrown into immediate and total poverty. Starvation was far from rare.

Many workers lived in the rapidly growing slums of cities like London and Manchester in England and New York and Boston in the United States. Their living conditions were often as bad as their working conditions.

There was rarely any sanitation, and little if any water. Under these conditions, it is not surprising that epidemics of various kinds were common in the slums.

The gulf between the factory owners and the factory workers was enormous. And it seemed to grow steadily as the Industrial Revolution went on. It can be summed up in one grim statistic: in some industries the life expectancy of the average worker was only one-half that of his or her employer.

## PSEUDO-DARWINISM

The inequalities of the situation were clear to everyone, from the unemployed textile worker to the wealthy factory owner. But the understanding of those inequities—of what they meant and what, if anything, should be done about them—differed greatly. Among those who benefited most from those inequities, the tendency was either to ignore them or to justify them.

Many of the more sensitive and concerned of the newly wealthy capitalists felt uncomfortable. They did not see themselves as being cruel, and yet they knew that the conditions their employees lived and worked under were cruel. And they profited from those conditions. In their effort to reconcile those two facts they appealed first to Adam Smith's "invisible hand." But Adam Smith himself had been unflattering toward those he referred to as the "masters." While he argued that their pursuit of self-interest at the expense of their "workmen" was necessary for the "invisible hand" to do its ultimately benevolent work, he had been harsh in his description of their methods.

Then, in 1859, another book was published which seemed to offer a scientific justification for what was taking place in the economic affairs of Britain and the United States. It was not intended to. It was not meant to deal with economics at all, but with biology. The book was written by a British naturalist named Charles Darwin and was called *On the Origin of Species by Means of Natural Selection*. It revolutionized the way in which people thought about the natural world, and it revolutionized the way in which many thought about economic activities as well.

Darwin argued that life in nature is a constant and endless struggle for survival. Different species of plants and animals are in desperate competition with each other, as are individual plants and animals. In this competition, some would survive and some would be destroyed.

In general, the species that survived were those that best managed to adapt themselves for the struggle through the process of biological evolution. This meant that over generations of development, those traits of individual members of a species which best helped them to succeed in the struggle for existence were passed on to their offspring, while those traits which hindered the species' survival were not. Some species evolved faster and more efficiently than others. Over time, these were the species that were victorious in the endless struggle. They survived. Darwin called this process "natural selection," but it became more widely known as "survival of the fittest."

Although Darwin was talking about biology, his book provided some people with a framework for understanding other aspects of life as well. By the end of the nineteenth century all kinds of pseudo-Darwinian theories were popular. The theory of biological evolution was used not only to explain but to justify such things as warfare (the ultimate form of the competition which was basic to survival) and even imperialism. According to what came to be known as "social Darwinism," imperialism was nothing more than the stronger and more perfectly evolved nations of the earth exerting their natural dominance over the weaker and less evolved nations.

A similar line of thought was used to justify even the harshest and most destructive effects of the growing concentration of economic power in the hands of a relatively few capitalists. Economic competition, it was argued, was merely an advanced form of the endless struggle for survival.

One of the most conspicuous victors in that endless struggle, the steel magnate Andrew Carnegie, summed it up best: "The price which society pays for the law of competition . . . is . . . great; but the advantages of this law are greater still, for it is to this law that we owe our wonderful material development, which brings improved conditions in its train. . . . (W)hile the law may be sometimes hard for the individual, it is best for the [human] race, because it insures the survival of the fittest in every department. We accept and welcome, therefore, as conditions to which we must accommodate ourselves, great inequality of environment, the concentration of business, industrial and commercial, in the hands of a few, and the law of competition between these, as being not only beneficial, but essential for the future progress of the race."

## CRITICS OF CAPITALISM

Others saw things differently. For them, it was impossible to justify the extreme inequality brought about under the new economic system either by an appeal to the "invisible hand" or to the "survival of the fittest." It seemed fundamentally wrong to them that the large number of

[43]

workers who provided the labor necessary for production should get so little, while the small number of entrepreneurs, who provided only the financial capital, should get so much.

These critics of the system began to refer to the entrepreneurs, rather contemptuously, as "capitalists," and to the system itself as "capitalism." Some saw the system as being seriously flawed, while others saw it as basically corrupt and oppressive.

The first group favored reforming the system, through legal or other measures to improve the lot of the laborers, while leaving the essential features of private ownership, competition, and free enterprise more or less intact. "Poor laws" were passed in England in 1834, for example, which established a national system of relief for the unemployed, but because they assumed the unemployed were at least partly responsible for their own plight, the relief offered was pitifully low. It was kept below the level earned by even the lowliest laborer, a level which in itself amounted to virtual poverty.

Other critics felt that such reforms could never correct the injustices that they saw as being an inevitable result of the capitalist system. What the capitalists considered productive self-interest, these critics saw as simple human greed. And when greed was made the chief motive force of society, they believed, large scale exploitation and poverty were bound to be the result.

At the heart of capitalism, they felt, was the object of that greed—private property. It was the ability of individuals to *own* things, and particularly to own the means of production—the capital goods, the things which were needed to produce other things—that allowed greed to function as the mainspring of economic activity. Many of the critics, then, came to believe that the only way to correct the inequities of capitalism was to attack the whole concept of private property. A Frenchman named Pierre Joseph Proudhon expressed it most succinctly (if paradoxically) when he declared simply: "Property is theft."

Some critics believed that all private property had to be done away with; others felt that it was enough to take the ownership of the means of production out of private hands. Some, known as syndicalists, favored turning the ownership of the factories over to the workers who worked in them. Others believed in the formation of cooperative communities, in which the ownership of the means of production would be shared by everyone within the community, workers and entrepreneurs alike. Still others argued that a democratic government should itself take over the ownership of the means of production and manage them for the benefit of the society as a whole.

While the various theories and plans advanced by these critics of capitalism were often in conflict with each other, the critics held certain beliefs in common. They all favored replacing at least some private ownership with some form of more general, social ownership. Because of this, they came to be called socialists, and their ideas, socialism.

## MARX AND ENGELS

By far the most influential critics of capitalism were two Germans, Karl Marx and Friedrich Engels. The two men met in Paris, where they wrote *The Communist Manifesto* together in 1848. Like 1776, the year in which *The Wealth of Nations* had been published, it was a year of revolution, and the *Manifesto* was a revolutionary document which called on the workers of the world to unite against what the authors considered their capitalist oppressors.

The two men later moved to England, where Marx, supported by his friend Engels (who had been a prominent capitalist himself) and by a poorly paid job as a newspaper correspondent for the *New York Tribune*, wrote a work called *Das Kapital*, the German phrase for "capital." Between them, these two men and these two works laid the foundation for much of modern socialist and Communist thought. That foundation has come to be known as Marxism.

Marxism holds that economic forces, including the ongoing and virtually unstoppable progress of technology, determine the course of history. That course is a kind of evolutionary process, and it is possible to predict, by examining the past and deducing the laws by which that evolution proceeds, where it is leading.

Much of Marx's thought had its roots in the theories of the so-called "classical" economists like Adam Smith. Like Smith, Marx believed in a labor theory of value. That is, he believed that the value of a commodity derived from the amount of labor needed to produce it. He went on to argue, however, that under capitalism, the workers never received in wages the equivalent of the value they put into the commodity they produced. The difference between the value they contributed and the wages they received was a "surplus value" which went to the capitalists.

Like Smith, too, Marx believed that competition— the conflict of self-interests—was a driving force of economic activity. But he saw the essential competition less in terms of private and individual self-interests than in

[46]

terms of the interests of the two great classes of the industrial age: the capitalist class (the bourgeoisie) and the working class (the proletariat). Since the bourgeoisie could only survive by taking the "surplus value" which had been rightfully earned by the proletariat's labor, the two classes were in fundamental conflict. Marx saw the process of historical evolution as the battle between these two classes. And that battle, he believed, would inevitably be won by the proletariat.

The victory of the proletariat was inevitable because only the labor of the proletariat could produce surplus value. Only their labor could produce the profits on which the capitalists depended—which were in fact, the whole purpose of the capitalists' existence. Marx believed that machinery was not capable of producing surplus value. While it could give one capitalist a competitive advantage over another by increasing efficiency, ultimately it could produce no more than its own value. So, to the extent that a capitalist invested more and more in machinery and less and less in the employment of workers, his rate of profit would fall. Since the march of technology was unstoppable (knowledge once learned could not be unlearned) and since competition would drive capitalists to make use of technology to achieve greater efficiency, the total rate of profit must inevitably fall. The resulting crisis would, according to Marxist belief, assure the destruction of the capitalists' power and the triumph of the proletariat.

When that happened, and the profit motive which controlled capitalist behaviors was removed, Marx believed that everyone would be better off. Goods would be produced and exchanged more efficiently, since there would be no surplus value sucked out of the process by

the unproductive capitalist class. What's more, the workers, who had been made miserable by the exploitation basic to capitalism, would become happy and self-fulfilled.

The ultimate goal of Marxism was a classless society, in which there would be little or no need of government, because there would be no need to protect one class from another. It would be, the Marxists believed, a modern society in which the wonders of technology would be the means of freeing people from the drudgery of the past. It would be a society in which everyone would work together, not for private profit but for mutual benefit—a goal summed up in the classic proclamation: "from each according to his abilities, to each according to his needs."

Since the victory of the proletariat, which would bring all this about, was historically inevitable as well as socially desirable, the Marxists believed, there was little point in trying to reform capitalist society. That would merely slow down the historical process. Better, perhaps, would be to encourage active revolution against the established order, thereby speeding the process along.

At heart, Marxism was a revolutionary philosophy. The capitalists and the workers, it argued, were locked into a mortal struggle by the economic forces of history. Finally, there could be no compromise. The proletariat must win, and in their victory the capitalist class must be destroyed. If this could be accomplished by violent revolution, so much the better.

*Karl Marx,*
*author of* Capital

# CONTRASTS

The two great economic ideals of capitalism and socialism still dominate economic thinking in the world today. The economic system of almost every developed country on earth is based on one or the other, or on some combination of them both.

Before going on to describe some of the actual economic systems that have evolved from these two competing ideals, it will be useful to examine some of the contrasting approaches each takes toward certain basic economic questions.

## ANSWERING QUESTIONS

In the Introduction to this book it was pointed out that every society has to answer three basic economic questions: what goods and services should the society produce? how should they be produced? and for whom should they be produced?

In actual practice, each of these very general questions breaks down into countless numbers of others. Should a factory be built to manufacture cars or razor blades? Should a garbage collector be paid more or less than a legal secretary? And so on. The specific answers any society will give to these practical questions will vary as much according to conditions and circumstances as they will according to the society's economic system. Given the same practical question, in fact, a capitalist society and a socialist society might come up with the same answer. (Both might decide that it was better to make more cars and fewer razor blades.) But the ways in which they go about making those decisions will differ.

A purely capitalist society would leave the answers to such questions to the workings of the marketplace— that is, to the millions upon millions of individuals, who are making decisions based on their own self-interest.

The question of what to produce (what kind of factory to build, for example) would be left to the private decisions of entrepreneurs. They would decide which enterprises they wanted to invest their capital in, based primarily on which might be expected to make them the biggest profit. Their decisions, in turn, would be influenced by the private decisions of the society's consumers who would decide, according to their own needs and wants, what they would be willing to pay for. Entrepreneurs would attempt to produce those things which sufficient numbers of people were willing to pay enough money for to make the enterprise profitable. The specific prices of the goods produced would vary according to the free actions of supply and demand in the marketplace.

A purely socialist society, on the other hand, would not allow such decisions to be made by private individuals, acting independently. Instead, the decisions would be made by some kind of collective body, based not on private self-interest but on the welfare of society as a whole.

The exact nature of the collective body would vary, depending on the brand of socialism being practiced. In a small socialist community or commune, such decisions might be made by all the members of the community meeting together. In a large nation, where such a meeting would be impractical, the decisions might be made by a governmental body either elected or appointed for the task. In practice (although many utopian socialists have argued in favor of small, independent communes), the latter alternative has been the rule in those nations which have adopted socialist economies. It has been found that, lacking free enterprise, competition, and the profit motive to drive the economy, a substantial amount of long-term and centralized economic planning has been necessary to give direction to economic development.

## THE QUESTION OF PROFIT

The right to private property is fundamental to the whole concept of capitalism. In order for the system to operate at all, people must be allowed to own things. They must be able to use their possessions more or less as they choose, and to dispose of them as they see fit. Those things that can be owned (including, but not limited to, money) make up an individual's wealth, and among the things he or she must be able to do with that wealth is to use it to generate more wealth. This process is the essence of the capitalism.

As might be expected, socialism rejects the central importance of the right to private property. In its most extreme form it rejects the concept of private property altogether, saying instead that property should be held collectively, by the community as a whole. The rights commonly associated with ownership—the rights to use and to dispose of property—should belong to the entire community, and should be exercised in the best interests of the entire community.

Many forms of socialism are not so extreme. They recognize the right to own certain forms of private property such as personal and household possessions, for example, and in some cases even houses and limited amounts of land. But virtually all forms of socialism insist on public (or collective) ownership of the means of production—the capital wealth which can be used to produce more wealth.

When the capitalist uses some of his or her wealth to produce more wealth, the new wealth thus generated also belongs to the capitalist. It is the capitalist's profit. It is the desire for this profit which, to a large extent, drives the market for goods and services that allows economic development to take place.

Capitalism holds that capitalists must be as free as possible to set up and conduct business enterprises in whatever ways they see fit in order to generate profits for themselves. To the extent that they are free to do so, capitalists believe, economic development will proceed at its fastest and most efficient pace and the entire society will ultimately benefit. To the extent that they are restricted or limited, the economic development of the society as a whole will suffer. The importance of freedom of enterprise is so basic to the functioning of capitalism, in fact, that the two terms, "capitalism" and "free enterprise" are often used interchangeably.

Socialism, however, holds that far from being the driving force of economic development, profit is an unnecessary and unjustified drain on that development. What's more, it is a device for taking a disproportionate amount of the wealth that rightfully should belong to society as a whole (and to everyone in society more or less equally) and giving it to a few individuals.

By insisting on the public ownership of the means of production, then, socialism aims at removing profit, and therefore the profit motive, from the economic process.

## SELF-INTEREST
## VERSUS ALTRUISM

In capitalist theory, the primary motivation for economic behavior is self-interest. This is as true for the worker as it is for the entrepreneur. Other motives —pride in accomplishment, the enjoyment of doing a particular task, and so forth—may play a part in the economic decisions of workers, and they may even be determining factors for some individuals. But most workers most of the time will make their economic decisions on the basis of self-interest, and they will usually see that self-interest in economic terms.

In an advanced capitalistic society this means that most workers will work in order to make money, for it is money that will enable them to buy what they want and need. The worker sells his labor in the marketplace in return for wages and other benefits (health insurance, vacation time, and so on) that can be expressed in terms of money.

In socialist theory, economic self-interest (and therefore money) is less important as a factor in motivating people to work. Money is still used as a medium of exchange, and workers may still be paid wages, but financial rewards play a much smaller role in allocating workers to jobs and jobs to workers. For one thing, the difference in pay between different kinds of jobs will usually be much smaller than under capitalism. For another, many of the benefits (pension plans, health insurance, and so forth) that in a capitalist society are considered part of the workers' wage-and-benefit package would, in a socialist society, be offered to all regardless of their job status.

The role played by economic self-interest in capitalism is replaced, in socialist theory, by a kind of social *altruism*. Altruism means the desire to help others, and in a socialist society workers are encouraged to see the work they do as benefiting all of society. This fact is considered to be, in and of itself, a significant psychological reward for work. Altruism exists in capitalist societies as well, of course, but it is rarely viewed as being central to the functioning of the economic system. While many capitalist businessmen pride themselves on the contributions their companies make to the well-being of society, those contributions are rarely the deciding factors in making business decisions. While many workers consider the social good brought about by their labor important, few consider it to be more important to them than their paychecks.

In capitalist theory, self-interest is the driving force behind economic progress; in socialist theory, self-interest is replaced by an equally driving force of cooperation for the common good.

## DIFFERENT CONCEPTS OF EQUALITY

Both capitalists and socialists claim to be egalitarian. That is, both believe that all members of society should be regarded, in some sense at least, as equals. And both believe that their society is best designed to promote that equality.

But capitalists and socialists view equality from very different perspectives. Capitalists are primarily concerned with the equality of individuals, and they see social equality as being mainly a question of equality of *opportunity*. For them, equality is largely a matter of individuals having an equal right to compete freely for personal economic advantage.

Some critics have argued that the opportunity to compete for economic advantage is not very meaningful in a society in which some people start out with great disadvantages. (One critic commented that such a right was the equivalent of the rich and the poor having the same opportunity to sleep under a bridge on a cold night.) But it has proven to be an extremely significant right to a great many people.

It has to be remembered that capitalism followed an age of feudalism, a time and a system in which people were doomed or privileged to live the exact kinds of economic lives their parents had lived. Capitalism was designed to free the economic energies of the privileged and the disadvantaged alike, and under it, in the nineteenth century, a great shift of wealth and power took place. A number of individuals who in an earlier age would have been doomed to lives of grinding poverty were enabled instead to amass great fortunes. If others remained trapped in the poverty they were born into, or fell into poverty, the capitalists believed that that was the price which had to be paid for the economic advancement of society as a whole.

Socialists approach the question of equality less from the perspective of the individual than from the perspective of class. They see equality less as a matter of opportunity than as a matter of result. Seeing the economic deprivation of individuals primarily as a function of the struggle between classes (the bad bourgeoisie against the good proletariat, as Marx presented it) socialists believe that the way to equality is to destroy class as a fact of economic and social life.

Socialism attempts to achieve its brand of equality first by removing the ownership of the means of production from private hands (the hands of a particular class) and placing it in the hands of the society as a whole. This shift in ownership makes the existence of a capitalist class unnecessary. (It does not, however, make the existence of *capital* unnecessary. It simply puts the ownership and control of capital in public rather than private hands.) The next step in achieving equality under socialism is achieved by distributing the wealth resulting from the production of goods more evenly among all members of society.

Absolute equality of goods seems to be unattainable, and even undesirable. Obviously, it would be wasteful, inefficient, and pointless to produce an equal number of each of the goods manufactured by a given society and to distribute an equal amount of each of them to every member of the society. Different people want and require different things. But movement toward more equal distribution of wealth to all members of the society is one of the major ideals of socialism.

That kind of economic equality, the equality of distribution, is not fundamental to the capitalist ideal, however. In fact, almost the exact opposite is true. Capitalism doesn't just accept the idea of economic inequality, it *requires* it. It is the possibility of achieving more than one's neighbors that provides the spur to the economic competition that is so central to the capitalist system.

[58]

# THE UNITED STATES — THE FACE OF CAPITALISM TODAY

Until now, we have been discussing the ideals of capitalism and socialism, the ideologies from which they sprang. But economic systems in the real world are never completely determined by ideology alone. They are shaped by national cultures, tradition, and specific circumstances. It is time now to look at two real economies, one capitalist and one socialist, and to see how they have actually evolved in practice.

Even more than Great Britain, where Adam Smith first observed the workings of the "invisible hand," it has been the United States in which the reality of modern capitalism has developed.

There are several reasons for this. One is that the birth of the United States, the first theories of capitalism, and the start of the Industrial Revolution occurred virtually simultaneously. The new country, freed from many of the class distinctions and traditions which were present in the Old World, was an ideal laboratory for the new economic experiment. Then, too, the continual westward expansion of the United States throughout its early history provided a unique opportunity for economic expansion. What's more, the democratic political ideas which were so much a part of the new country's founding ideology were ideally suited to the capitalistic ideas of economic freedom and competitive enterprise.

In the United States, the capitalist ideal represented an opening up of economic opportunity to a greater proportion of the new nation's population than had ever been attempted anywhere before, just as the democratic ideal represented an opening up of political opportunity. The two experiments of capitalism and democracy, going forward together, proved, to a large extent, to be mutually nourishing, and produced the leading capitalist nation in the world today. That modern capitalist reality, however, is somewhat different from the model presented by Adam Smith and other early advocates of classical capitalism. In this chapter, we will explore some of those differences.

## GOVERNMENT REGULATION

Perhaps the most striking differences between the capitalist model as presented by Adam Smith and the reality of American capitalism today have to do with the extent to which the government of the United States is involved in the economic affairs of its citizens.

The capitalist distaste for government regulation of business activity has been a staple of American political ideology from the beginning. And yet, American history has seen a long and almost steady increase in such government regulation. Today every major industry in the country, and most small businesses, are affected to some degree or other by regulation from local, state, and federal governments.

This has not, by and large, been the result of any major ideological change. It is probably still widely believed that there should be as little regulation as possible. It is just that over the years, on a case by case basis, more and more such regulation has become generally acknowledged as necessary.

Pressure for regulation has come largely from two sources. The first is the public, consumers of the products and services of the industries being regulated. The second is industry itself. The reasons behind consumer pressures for regulation are obvious. Consumers wish to be protected from unfair or deceptive business practices, and from defective or unsafe products.

The reasons for industry pressures on behalf of greater regulation may be less clear. But the fact is that a number of industries have, at one time or another, seen themselves as benefiting from government regulation. Although government regulation may in some respects limit a company's freedom to compete in the marketplace, it can also sometimes protect the company against the negative effects of that competition.

This is particularly true of companies that are granted monopolies. A monopoly is an exclusive right or ability to provide a certain product or service in a particular market. Monopolies are desirable from a business's point of view because they eliminate competition from other companies. (Some monopolies are partial: generally, any company having 80 percent of the market is considered to have a monopoly.) Sometimes a company achieves a monopoly by having sole control of an important invention. Being the only company with the knowledge, or the patent, to produce a certain product, it is able to control the market. But other monopolies are granted to a company by the government.

Such government-granted monopolies usually involve a trade-off. The government awards the monopoly in return for a significant amount of regulatory authority over the company's business. A monopoly of this kind is rare and is usually granted only to a company which provides an essential service to the public, a utility providing electricity or water, for example, to a given community or region.

In such cases, the business argues that it needs the monopoly, and the assured market that goes with it, in order to justify the enormous capital expenditures needed to start up and maintain such a vital service. Governments are willing to grant the monopoly in order to assure (through the regulatory power they claim in exchange), that the utility will provide the service to all members of the community at a fair price. Thus both the business and the government (representing the public) feel that they have something to gain from the arrangement.

While virtually no American industry is totally exempt from government regulation, some are more heavily affected by it than others. Many of the major transportation industries (railroads, airline, and trucking companies) have been subjected to large-scale regulation of routes, rates, and safety procedures. The communications industries of radio and television fall under regulatory authority because they use a publicly owned resource (the airwaves) to conduct their business. (The government's authority to regulate program content, however, is severely limited by the Constitutional guarantee of freedom of speech.) The food and drug industries are subject to strict health and safety standards. The banking and finance industries, custodians of the savings of the American public, are subject to a wide range of controls on what they can and can not do with them.

The Stock Exchange on Wall Street in
New York is regulated by the Securities
and Exchange Commission (SEC).

In addition to the specific regulations affecting these and other industries, there are general laws and regulations concerning fair business practices, employee safety, stock sales, and other matters that affect businesses in all industries.

In recent years the trend toward ever-increasing regulation of industry by government has been slowed, and perhaps even reversed. This change began to take place under the administration of President Jimmy Carter, which took major steps to deregulate the airline and trucking industries despite loud protests from the industries themselves. It has continued, and even accelerated, under the administration of Ronald Reagan.

## GOVERNMENT HELP
## TO INDUSTRY

Another important departure from the principle of *laissez-faire* is the granting of certain benefits by government to industry. These include tax breaks given to certain businesses in return for their doing things the government feels are socially desirable—for employing more people, for example, or investing in more productive machinery.

In some cases, these benefits take the form of outright government subsidies. A subsidy is a payment made by the government for which the government gets nothing directly in return. It is a kind of gift given by the government in the expectation that it will ultimately benefit society as a whole.

An early example of such a government subsidy to industry was the granting of huge quantities of public lands to the railroad companies of the nineteenth century. The government wanted railroads built across the country, and wanted to encourage people to settle in the west. In order to promote these socially desirable goals, the government made gifts of lands to the railroad companies. The railroads sold the land to raise the capital for the building project. The government received no interest in the railroads in return. Many of the people who bought the land were farmers and other settlers who moved west to live on it.

Today, the government continues to subsidize certain industries in a number of ways. One of the most notable of these industries is agriculture, which receives a variety of price supports and other subsidies, including payments to farmers to plant certain crops, or not to plant any crops at all. These subsidies are given not in order to generate income for the government, or even in an altruistic effort to help the farmers. They're given in order to assure the health of the farm industry, and thus to assure a steady supply of food to the American population.

Some of the most recent and controversial government subsidies have been those granted to certain specific corporations in order to "bail them out" of financial difficulties. These corporations have included Lockheed (a major supplier of military equipment to the government) and Chrysler Corporation (now the fourteenth largest corporation in the country) among others. The government granted these companies loans, or loan guarantees, at favorable interest rates in order to assure their financial survival. Many conservative capitalists objected to these loans as government interference in the economic affairs of business, but the government argued that they were necessary. Their purpose, according to government spokesmen, was not to help the individual businesses as such, but to help the many people and oth-

Chrysler President Lee Iacocca shakes
hands with President Jimmy Carter
after Carter signed the Chrysler aid bill.

er businesses who were dependent on them. That is, to help the society, and the economy, as a whole.

## TAXATION

The most direct form of government involvement in the financial affairs of its citizens is taxation. The federal government has a great range of financial responsibilities, from providing for the national defense to the construction of interstate highways. State governments have many financial responsibilities of their own, as do such other levels of government as counties and cities. Some of these expenses can be met through fees for services (such as postal fees, tolls, and the like) but the bulk of them have to be met through the imposition of taxes of one kind or another.

Taxes take many forms. There are sales taxes, levied in many states on the retail sales of most goods; excise taxes, levied on particular goods such as gasoline, tobacco, and alcohol; tariffs on imported goods; and inheritance taxes imposed on the estates of people after death. But the largest single tax imposed in the United States is the federal income tax. This tax is levied on both individuals and corporations, and consists of a proportion of their net incomes. It is a progressive tax, which means that the proportion of income taken by the government grows as the amount of net income grows. The effect of this is to assure that those people and businesses with higher incomes pay not only a greater *amount* in taxes than those with lesser incomes, but that they pay a greater *percentage* of their incomes as well. Proponents of the progressive income tax argue that it is only fair that those who are better able to pay are required to pay at a higher rate than those with less income. Opponents argue that the progressive tax is economically counterproductive since it takes a higher proportion of money out of the hands of those who would be most likely to invest their money in productive economic activity.

In addition to the federal taxes, states, cities, and other jurisdictions levy a variety of taxes of their own. Most states levy income and excise taxes and many levy sales taxes as well. Cities rely heavily on property taxes imposed on real estate, and some also have their own sales and/or income taxes.

The amounts collected in all these taxes are enormous. In 1982, for example, the federal personal income tax bill in the United States added up to $298,111,000,000; the federal income tax on corporations came to $49,207,000,000. Social insurance taxes and contributions added up to another $180,000,000,000, while other federal insurance and retirement taxes and contributions came to more than $20,446,000,000. Altogether, the Federal Internal Revenue Service collected some $632,200,000,000 that year, a total which has been climbing in the years since. (In 1983, the last year for which figures are available, state and local governments collected some $478,200,000,000 of their own.) Even with all this money coming in, the federal government has been sinking deeper and deeper into debt for years, and finds itself forced to borrow billions of dollars to meet its expenditures.

The collection of these enormous sums in taxes, combined with the even more enormous expenditures of governments at all levels, has the effect of redirecting vast amounts of capital away from the channels in which it would otherwise flow. The considerations of governments in deciding where and how to spend money are often very different from those of private individuals and businesses. The great financial power wielded by governments is very different from the forces of private competition assumed by the classical capitalist economists. Clearly, the very authority that governments have to compel certain kinds of economic behavior and to forbid others distorts the free-market competition which would (according to those economists) allow the "invisible hand" to do its most effective work.

Yet, despite the general belief in capitalism in the United States, these distortions have been accepted as necessary by the majority of the public. While there is a great deal of controversy over particular taxes, and over the amount of taxation as a whole, most people recognize the need for massive government expenditures and for the compulsory taxes necessary to finance them.

## PUBLIC OWNERSHIP

As we have seen, the federal, state, and even municipal governments exert a good deal of control over American business through a combination of regulation, taxation, and various forms of incentives and subsidies. But for the most part they have been willing, even eager, to leave the actual ownership and management of businesses in private hands.

There have been (and are) exceptions. Transportation systems in many areas are owned and operated by local or state governments. Mail service in the United States was run by a cabinet department of the federal government until 1970, when the post office was reorganized as the United States Postal Service. Since that time, it has been run more like a private business while it remains an agency of the federal government.

Perhaps the biggest single deviation from the capitalist rule of private ownership of business came with the formation of the Tennessee Valley Authority (TVA) in 1933. A corporate agency of the federal government, the TVA has the job of overseeing the development of the vast Tennessee Valley region, an area of more than 40,000 square miles in the American middle south. The generally recognized success of the TVA in carrying out this huge assignment (despite criticisms that label the agency "socialist") led to the establishment of a number of similar, although less ambitious, projects elsewhere in the country.

But these examples are exceptions to the general rule. Overall there has been an extreme reluctance on the part of governments at all levels to take on ownership of any economic institution which could conceivably be run as a private business. Still, while the capitalist restraint on public (government) ownership of industry has been very strong throughout this nation's history, such examples as the TVA and the various public transit authorities demonstrate it has been far from absolute.

## HELPING THE DISADVANTAGED

One of the issues that every society must face is how to provide for those members of the society who cannot provide for themselves. That issue is particularly acute in capitalist societies, where the system of economic competition implies that the advantages gained by some will come at the expense of others.

For a long time in the United States, the solution to the problem was assumed to be the responsibility of private charity. Churches and other altruistic organizations were given the job of helping the poor and otherwise disadvantaged.

The reliance on private charity proved unsatisfactory, however. For one thing, it was haphazard and uncoordinated, which meant that while some people might be quite well served, others would be ignored totally. This kind of unequal treatment ran counter to a basic American sense of fairness.

Finally, when the Great Depression of the 1930s threw millions and millions of people out of work and into poverty, a consensus developed that it was necessary for the government to do something.

The result was a variety of federal programs, known as the New Deal, designed to help the disadvantaged. Chief among them was Social Security, which inaugurated both a federal unemployment insurance program and an old-age pension plan.

In the years since the New Deal, and notably during the 1960s, more federal programs have been added. Along with a greatly expanded Social Security program, these include Medicare, to provide medical care for the nation's elderly; Medicaid, to provide similar care for the poor; Aid to Families with Dependent Children, to provide a minimum of support for the children of the poor; food stamps, to help the economically disadvantaged to buy food (and not incidentally to help the producers of food); and a number of others. All the states and many cities and counties have similar programs of their own.

Almost all of these programs have been controversial. But, despite the controversy, the majority of Americans seem to have accepted the idea that the government has a necessary role to play in assisting the disadvantaged. The only remaining questions are those regarding the size of that role.

## DEFICIT SPENDING

The Great Depression also prompted a new government role in directing the national economy. For the first time, the government began to use its spending power not merely to purchase goods and services, but to promote employment and business activity.

Previously, the government had made expenditures to meet specific needs and had attempted to raise the money to pay for those expenditures as quickly thereafter as possible. If it had sometimes fallen into debt (deficit), that condition had been unintentional and regarded as unfortunate.

But in the 1930s, in an effort to do something about the terrible Depression which was crippling the national economy and forcing tens of millions of people into poverty, the government began to take on deficits deliberately. In doing so, it was following the theories of an English economist named John Maynard Keynes. He argued that in times of economic depression massive government deficits were not bad for the economy but good for it. By spending more money than it took in through taxes, the government would be adding money into the economic system. This would promote business activity and result in more jobs for the workers. This would not just help businessmen and the particular workers who got the new jobs, it would help the entire economy. Later, once the economy was sufficiently restored to prosper without any new injections of money from the federal government, taxes could be raised to pay off the accumulated debt.

[72]

Keynes's views ran counter to the traditional policies of *laissez-faire* capitalism, but they were nonetheless largely adopted by the government of President Franklin Roosevelt, and they have been occasionally followed by other administrations since. Even Ronald Reagan, who has spoken out strongly against deficit spending as a deliberate policy, presided during his first term as president over an economic recovery that many economists say was financed by huge federal deficits.

## THE STRENGTH OF LABOR

There has been a tremendous evolution in the status and power of the labor sector of the American economy over the course of the nation's history. When the country was founded, as we have seen, management had a built-in advantage in its competition with labor. That advantage was seen by Adam Smith, among others, as unfortunate but inevitable. Political as well as financial power was all on the side of management (or, as Smith put it, the "masters"). Laws forbade workers to organize to increase their power, yet no laws forbade the "masters" to do the same.

The very first labor union in the new United States was founded as early as 1792, but it was small and ineffective. It was also, of course, illegal—or at least it was widely believed to be so. Common law forbade "conspiracy" and courts usually held that forming a union amounted to a "conspiracy" against the employers. It wasn't until 1842 that a Judge Shaw of the Massachusetts State Supreme Court ruled that union activity did not, after all, constitute an illegal conspiracy, and that it was therefore legal to form unions in the United States.

[73]

Even so, the struggle of labor to organize and compete effectively with management was long and hard, and sometimes violent. In some industries, such as steel and coal mining, virtual wars were fought between union members and "private police" hired by the companies over the right of the workers to organize and bargain collectively.

Eventually, the workers won that right, and in the years since, the efforts of organized labor have had a profound effect on the economic system. Largely because of the unions, child labor has been forbidden, the safety of working conditions (once entirely a matter of company policy) has become subject to regulation, working hours have been limited, minimum wages have been mandated by law for several industries, and many more reforms have taken place. And, of course, workers in many industries have, through collective bargaining, won for themselves a much bigger slice of the economic pie in the form of wages and benefits.

In short, the relative power of labor and management has been put into much closer balance. In the mid-1970s, the AFL-CIO, the largest labor organization in America, claimed a membership of between 13 and 14 million. Organized labor's influence in American politics, and particularly in the affairs of the Democratic Party, has been great. Some businessmen claim, in fact, that the combined economic and political power of organized labor has grown so great that it is in danger of upsetting the balance of interests which is the special genius of capitalism.

Representatives of organized labor, on the other hand, claim that this is not true. They say that in reality the balance is still very much weighted on the side of management. They point out that about 75 percent of

American workers remain unorganized (although the percentage of workers legally allowed to join unions and have not done so is much lower), and they add that, as a result of recent bouts of inflation and recession, union membership has actually been declining. They argue further that even many union members have been forced to accept pay cuts and losses in fringe benefits in recent contract negotiations.

In any case, there is no question but that organized labor has become a major factor in the American economy.

## THE POWER OF
## THE LARGE CORPORATIONS

Along with the rise in the power of organized labor has come an even greater rise in the power of the large corporation. The economic landscape of Adam Smith's time was studded with tradesmen, farmers, merchants, and industrial entrepreneurs. But they were, with very few exceptions, what would today be called small businessmen.

They could, and did, band together and pool some of their resources in joint stock companies, but even such combinations were relatively small. Except when they were given monopolies, they were subject to competition from similar combinations which were relatively easily formed. The largest of them were quite small compared to the giant corporations of today.

A corporation is a legal entity. Like the joint stock companies of the mercantilist period, it is chartered by a government (in the United States, usually a state government). Unlike the companies of an earlier time, however, it is not expected to act on the government's behalf, but only on the behalf of its own stockholders. Among the advantages of incorporating is a limitation on the financial liability of the investors in the corporation. Their risk is limited to the amount of money they invest, and this limitation makes it easier for the company to attract investors.

Each investor receives stock in the company, the amount depending on how much money he or she puts in. The effective control and management of the company, however, is usually kept in the hands of a small group.

The largest of today's corporations control amounts of capital and resources greater than those of many countries. The single largest corporation in America in 1982, for example, had $97 billion in sales and profits of over $4 billion. Even the twenty-first largest had sales of over $13 billion and profits of nearly $1.9 billion. It has been estimated that despite the fact that there are more than one million corporations in the United States today, a mere 100 of them control fully one half of the corporate wealth in the entire country.

The economic power wielded by such corporations is enormous. In their ability to influence, and even to dominate, the market in many goods, their power is far beyond anything dreamt of by Adam Smith. There is a great deal of concern today, among many traditional capitalists as well as among socialists, about the vast size and power of these economic giants. The capitalists worry about the degree to which this concentration of economic power distorts the forces of effective competition, and deflects the workings of the "invisible hand."

Despite all these—and many other—differences from the classical model of capitalism as envisaged by Adam

Smith, the basic elements of capitalism remain firmly in place in the United States today.

While there is substantial government regulation of industry, the bulk of the means of production remain in private hands. While there is a great deal of taxation, the accumulation of private wealth is still possible—and that possibility still serves as an important motive for economic activity. While there is significant government help available for the economically disadvantaged, government assistance is far from being so great that it removes the incentive for private economic activity. So, although the government has taken a major role in a wide variety of economic areas, the free market forces of supply, demand, and competition still dominate the marketplace.

# THE SOVIET UNION — ONE FACE OF SOCIALISM TODAY

## NONREVOLUTIONARY SOCIALISTS

Once the conclusion had been reached that capitalism had to be replaced with a fairer and less cruel system, the socialists faced the question of how the change could be brought about.

Some believed that the change could only come through revolution—the violent overthrow of the capitalist system which they saw as dominating the western world. The capitalists, they argued, who controlled the wealth of society, would not give up their wealth (or their power) willingly. It would have to be taken from them by force. These nineteenth-century revolutionary socialists tended to be believers in the teachings of Karl Marx, and their efforts would reach an early climax in the Russian Revolution of 1917.

But not all those who considered themselves socialists, or even Marxists, believed in the necessity of revolution. (Even Marx himself suggested that socialism might be achieved peacefully in some societies.) Many socialist movements and parties believed in the peaceful advance of socialism. Important among these were the

Christian Socialists, who identified the communal and unselfish values of socialism with the teachings of Christ. Most of the nonrevolutionary socialists called themselves "democratic socialists." At least in countries with long-standing democratic traditions like England and the United States, they believed that the best route to socialism was by gradually reforming the capitalist system. By educating the working class to the benefits of socialism and appealing to the fairness of enlightened members of the bourgeoisie, they believed reforms could be introduced through democratic processes. Socialist values, and eventually socialist institutions, would eventually spread through all of western society.

Organizations such as Britain's Fabian Society, led by Sydney and Beatrice Webb and the famous playwright George Bernard Shaw, were formed to spread socialist ideas. Ironically, their efforts were often most successful among members of the middle class rather than among the proletariat who were expected to be most attracted to them.

Political parties representing virtually every brand of socialism were formed throughout Europe, and eventually in the United States as well. Rivalry among the various socialist movements was often as bitter as that between the socialists and the capitalists. But by the turn of the twentieth century, if not before, it was clear that the major ideological conflict in the western world was that between socialism and capitalism—between the two great visions of economic reality put forward by Karl Marx and Adam Smith.

## THE RUSSIAN REVOLUTION

Marx's revolutionary theories were given their first great practical test in 1917, when a socialist-communist revolution overthrew the centuries-old government of imperial Russia.

That government had been an oddity among the major governments of the twentieth century. It had been essentially feudal, operating in much the same way as it had in the Middle Ages. The majority of Russia's population had been peasants, living in poverty, while the nation's nobility had lived on a lavish scale. The government had been headed for more than three centuries (since 1613) by the Romanovs, a family of hereditary tsars and tsarinas, many of whom had ruled with barbaric cruelty.

The new government established after the revolution was committed to socialism. Its leaders saw that system as being the only one that could right the wrongs caused by centuries of oppression suffered by the vast majority of Russia's population. In 1922, Russia united with several of its less powerful neighbors to form the Union of Soviet Socialist Republics, a union clearly dominated by Russia itself. The new country thus formed conducted the world's first major national experiment in socialism.

The Soviet Union's brand of socialism, however, was not that which had been imagined by the Christian Socialists or by the Fabian Society. Growing out of the Russian tradition of autocratic and dictatorial rule, and shaped by the violence of revolution, it was a totalitarian brand of socialism, imposed ruthlessly by a small group of leaders.

The revolution had been conducted by a number of political groups and parties. In its aftermath, one party, known as the Bolsheviks, forced their way to power over the other, more moderate, socialists. They called themselves the Communist party, and once having seized power they quickly turned the Soviet Union into a one-party state. Once in charge, they set out on the huge task of socializing the largely traditional, manorial-feudal economy of the largest country in the world.

The socialization was limited at first. The New Economic Policy, established in 1921 just before the union, allowed for some private ownership. It even allowed for some typically capitalist incentives to promote productivity in the agricultural and industrial sectors of Russia's economy. By 1928, however, the Communist party was ready to complete the transformation to socialism. Under the leadership of Joseph Stalin, a series of "Five-Year Plans" were instituted. These plans were blueprints for the economic development of the nation. They were pure examples of command economy—government directives spelling out what should be produced, how it should be produced, and how it should be distributed.

The early Five-Year Plans had two main goals: first, to industrialize Russia (which was still an almost entirely agricultural nation) and second, to collectivize Russia's farms.

Both of these goals were effectively achieved, but at a terrible cost. The industrialization of the Soviet economy was accomplished in a surprisingly short time, but it was done by concentrating on heavy industry. The production of the kinds of consumer goods which would have directly improved the life of the citizens of the Soviet Union was largely ignored.

There were two main reasons for this. The first was military. With a revolutionary socialist government facing a capitalist Europe, the nation felt itself besieged by enemies on all sides. The development of heavy industry increased its strength. The second reason was nationalistic. The new Communist leaders of Russia were, despite their ideology, as Russian at heart as the rulers they had overthrown. The production of great machines and the demonstration of military power allowed them to demonstrate to the world that Russia was the industrial equal of any nation on the continent.

The collectivization of the farms was accomplished at an even greater, and much bloodier, cost. The Russian peasants, who had suffered for centuries under the tsars, had dreamed of economic independence after the revolution. They had expected to get the ownership of the land that their families had worked, as near slaves, for centuries. But the new government robbed them of that dream. Instead of owning their own land, the peasants simply underwent a change of masters—from the local noble to the Communist state. Several million of the peasants rebelled. They slaughtered their cattle in defiance of the orders of the government.

The strength of their anger is reflected in the fact that during the course of the forced collectivization almost half of the 67 million cattle in the Soviet Union were killed. More terribly, seven million peasants died as well. Some five million peasant households were eliminated altogether. Millions of the peasants died during the famine that followed the agricultural chaos, and millions more were killed in the forced labor camps to which they were sent by the government.

The collectivization was successful, however, in the sense that it resulted in a rapid mechanization of Soviet agriculture and improved the efficiency of agricultural production.

At the same time, progress was being made in other sectors of the economy. Under the tsars, the vast majority of the population had received little in the way of health care or other social services. Under the new government, these services were provided free. Such mea-

*The collectivization of Soviet agriculture mechanized the farms in a short time. In this 1930s photo workers head out to the fields on tractors rented from the Machine and Tractor station near Moscow. In the early years of collectivization, such stations provided local collectives with modern equipment.*

sures of social progress as literacy levels advanced dramatically. Although these advances had been brought about at a terrible cost in blood and political repression, there is no question that the advances were both real and widespread.

## THE ROLE
## OF THE WORKERS

If the ideal of revolutionary socialism was to produce a classless society, that ideal seems to have been abandoned by the Soviet Communists sometime in the 1930s. If the ideal was to establish a society in which the proletariat (the workers, who according to Marxist theory produced the wealth of the entire society) were the elite, that ideal seems to have been abandoned as well.

In reality, the workers are at the bottom of the Soviet economic scale. Just as in most capitalist societies, management personnel receive much more in both pay and privileges than the workers they manage. At the top of the society are the true elite of the Soviet Union: a mixture of Communist party officials; leading industrial executives; scientists; military leaders; renowned artists, performers, and world class athletes. It is felt that these are the individuals who do the most for the Soviet state, and in a totalitarian country that is the most important consideration.

It is difficult to make precise comparisons between the relative economic positions of groups in the Soviet Union and their counterparts in the United States. The societies, expectations, and resources are so different that in many ways conditions are simply not comparable at all. Still, it is probably fair to say that the gulf between the standards of living of those at the top and those at the bottom of Soviet society are not as great as the cor-responding gulf between top and bottom in the United States. But it is also probably fair to say that such differences have tended to narrow in the United States over the past several decades, while they have stayed wide— or even widened—in the Soviet Union. It is also certainly fair to say that, by western standards at least, the average person in the United States is significantly better off than the average citizen of the Soviet Union.

Like workers in the United States, many workers in the Soviet Union belong to organizations referred to as unions. But the role of unions in the Soviet Union is very different. In the United States unions are expected to represent one economic group, their members, in a competition with other economic groups. Unions are, in a sense, the representatives of a special interest battling with other special interests for a larger share of the economic pie.

In the Soviet Union, however, unions are not expected to compete against other elements of society. In the Soviet Union, under Communist theory, the workers rule. The interests of the workers and the interests of the state are considered to be the same. There can be no competition for advantage, since there is no conflict of interest. Since the interest of the state is to meet the economic goals set by the government, the role of the unions is to promote those goals. Instead of protecting workers against unreasonable demands, the unions are agents of those demands. Instead of representing the workers in disputes with management (which in the Soviet Union means with the government) unions are representatives of the government. Despite the Communist theory, of course, there are often conflicts between the interests of the workers and the interests of the state, but in those conflicts the workers cannot look to their unions for help. In fact, when it comes to such conflicts, the unions are expected to help keep the workers in line.

## MOVING TOWARD CAPITALISM?

The Soviet government made a deliberate decision, early in its existence, to socialize virtually every aspect of the Soviet economy. After the brief tolerance of certain capitalist practices under the New Economic Policy, an effort was made to remove such traces of capitalism from every corner of Soviet life. At the same time, it was decided that the interests of the state required that the industrial development of the country would be concentrated in the areas of heavy industry, which would increase the state's power, and not in the areas of consumer goods, which would raise the standard of living of its citizens.

In recent decades, there has been some movement away from these early decisions. In the 1960s, for example, a determination was made to increase the production of consumer appliances, a branch of production which had been all but ignored previously. In 1960, there were less than half a million refrigerators being produced in the Soviet Union. By 1981, some 4.6 million were being produced. Also in 1960, the Soviets produced less than 2 million television sets; by 1981, they were producing almost 8.2 million. This greater concentration on consumer goods has continued into the present decade.

Even more dramatic are recent efforts to insert capitalist incentives into the Soviet economy, and to move

Soviet leader Mikhail Gorbachev's visit
to an automobile factory points up the
recent concentration on consumer goods.

away from the extremely centralized planning that characterized the early years of the Soviet Union's existence.

In recent decades, the government has allowed members of agricultural collectives the right to work a small piece of land in their own economic interest. While the crops from the collective as a whole have to be sold to the government, at prices determined by the government, the produce from this small piece of land can be sold at special markets, at prices determined by the forces of supply and demand. This not only enables the farmer to supplement his otherwise meager earnings from the collective, but it enables his customers to supplement their otherwise limited diet.

While the socialist ideal was that all should contribute to the society to the best of their ability, and in return receive from the society what they needed, the Soviet reality is somewhat different. Indeed, in a number of fields, workers are encouraged to work more productively by such capitalistic rewards as higher pay and better fringe benefits.

In the areas of industrial planning and management, too, there has been a noticeable shift away from the country's command economy beginnings. More and more, management decisions which used to be made by a central agency of the government are being made by the management personnel on the spot.

This is not to say that the Soviets have adopted a western-model capitalist system, where individual factory managements make their decisions based on the market forces of competition and supply and demand. Far from it. The government still sets the economic goals. The government still decides what will be produced, and still sets strict quotas of sales (and even of acceptable profit margins) that must be met. It is only within these government-set guidelines that individual managements are starting to receive a certain leeway. They do not set the goals, but they are winning more freedom to decide how those goals can best be met. When some institutions actually exceed the goals set by the government, capitalist incentives may be activated. Both management and workers in those specific industries are eligible to receive bonuses. The effect of these capitalist-style incentives has been to promote competition and efficiency in the manufacturing process.

Despite these moves in what seems to be a capitalist direction, the Soviet Union is still very much a Communist society. The means of production, including all of the land, are owned by the state. It is ultimately the state, and not private citizens, which decides the answers to the fundamental economic questions of what goods shall be produced, how they shall be produced, and for whom. In the light of these basic realities, the small movements in the direction of capitalist practices are relatively insignificant. There is, however, a recognition on the part of the Soviet leadership that the forces of self-interest, competition, and supply and demand still have their power. And there is another recognition as well: that any government effort to abolish those forces altogether—even with all the power and repression at the Soviet government's command—is destined to fail.

# OTHER
# ECONOMIES

In this book we have been primarily concerned with the two dominant economic ideologies in the world today, capitalism and socialism. We have examined their origins and discussed what each stands for. We have looked at the two largest and most powerful national economies in the world, each of which has evolved from one of these ideologies—that of the United States, which is the best example available of how a modern capitalist economic system works, and that of the Soviet Union, the world's first large-scale experiment with socialism.

Although each of these national economies was based on one of the two ideologies, neither is a pure example of the ideology from which it grew. Each has been changed and reshaped, both by the cultural traditions of the nation itself and by the forces of circumstance and particular events. Many economists would even deny that they are true examples of either capitalism or socialism.

In a sense, those economists are right. But in another sense, the United States is very much a capitalist country, and the Soviet Union is very much a socialist one. They are examples of *real* capitalist and socialist economies and not merely *theoretical* ones. They are examples of ways in which such economic systems develop in the real world, a world in which the evidence suggests that no ideologically pure economic system can exist for long. The forces of culture and pragmatism are too strong.

It is important, however, to realize that these are not the only ways in which economies can develop in the real world. Capitalism, for example, was born in Great Britain, and it has evolved in a significantly different form there than it has in the United States. Socialism has taken on very different forms in many Third World countries than it has in the Soviet Union. Even the communism of China, every bit as dictatorial and totalitarian as that of the Soviet Union, is in many respects hardly recognizable as an offshoot of the same ideology.

Most countries in the western world, in fact, are not exclusively committed to either capitalism or socialism. For the most part, they combine elements of both. They are pragmatic. When faced with an economic question, they look for an answer that works. They are not overly concerned with being ideologically consistent, only with solving the specific problem at hand.

In the Soviet Union there is only one political party, the Communist party, and it is ideologically committed to its particular brand of socialism. In the United States, there are two main political parties, but each of them is ideologically committed to some form of capitalism, however modified. In most western countries, however, there are major socialist as well as capitalist political parties, sometimes a number of each. Parties of both camps have significant political strength within each of the countries. Parties of both camps occasionally win elections and form governments. When capitalists are in

[92]

power, they institute capitalist measures, and when the socialists are in power they institute socialist measures.

In most of these countries, both sides have tended to move fairly slowly, even when they were in power. In order to avoid the economic dislocations that would result from attempting to set up an entirely new economic system every time the government changes hands, they have practiced the art of compromise.

The result has been economies in which capitalist and socialist elements exist side by side, and even combine. Sometimes they clash, but sometimes they blend surprisingly well and function efficiently together.

Perhaps the leading example of this kind of truly mixed economy is that of Sweden. Unlike some of the other mixed economies in Europe, Sweden's was the result of a deliberate choice. The Swedish, faced with a choice between capitalism and socialism, set out to find what they call a "middle way" to economic stability and prosperity.

This effort was begun in the midst of the Great Depression of the 1930s. In that decade, the socialist Social Democrat party came to power. Although they have won most of the elections since, they have rarely held an overwhelming majority. Essentially moderates in any case, the Social Democrats led Sweden on a road of compromise. They initiated a political-economic course which combined the long-standing Swedish tradition of the private ownership of business with a substantial amount of governmental direction of the economy. To this combination they added an extraordinarily far-reaching and generous welfare system.

The Swedish "middle way" has been a tremendous success when judged by objective economic measures.

One of the poorest countries in Europe in the early twentieth century, Sweden has since become one of the most prosperous countries in the entire world. With the highest per capita income of any country in Europe, Sweden seems to have proved that a mixed economy can function every bit as well as one that follows a single ideology.

## THE WORLD ECONOMY

Capitalist, moderate socialist, Communist, and mixed economies of all kinds share the world economy together. With however much difficulty, they are forced to deal with each other.

Even such ideologically and politically hostile nations as the United States and the Soviet Union find themselves trading with each other. The Soviets, for example, have occasionally bought huge amounts of grain from the United States, particularly when the grain harvest in the Soviet Union has been poor. This is something of an embarrassment for the Soviet Union, and it is also something of an embarrassment for many American grain farmers, who as a group are extremely anti-Communist. But the Soviet Union's embarrassment does not stop it from buying the needed grain; and the farmers' embarrassment does not stop them from selling it.

Some ideologically committed countries have tried to insulate their economies from the rest of the world. Perhaps the most extreme example of this was that of the People's Republic of China. Following the Communist revolution there in 1949, the new government tried to make the Chinese economy self-sufficient. It hid its economy behind the Great Wall of China as though the

An American expert helps Chinese technicians
install equipment from the United States.

Wall could somehow protect its brand of extreme communism from the economic contamination of capitalist influences. But even China has recently come to realize her economic interdependence with the rest of the world. This most rigidly anti-capitalist of all anti-capitalist nations has had an "opening to the West." The Communist government of China has even entered into partnerships with western, capitalist corporations to build factories in China. It has purchased large quantities of cigarettes from an American tobacco company, and negotiated for the purchase of American soft drinks.

As can be seen from these examples, even the most extremely ideological governments are subject to the influence of economic pragmatism. When the reality of the situation called for it, even such an ideologically committed government as that of China proved willing not only to deal with capitalist governments, but to ally itself with capitalist corporations. By the same token, these capitalist corporations have proven perfectly willing—and even eager—to deal with them.

The economic wants of the people of the world are real. Societies will inevitably attempt to meet those wants by means of their economic systems. As we have seen in this book, the role of ideology in the formation of these economic systems is very important and must not be underestimated. At the same time, the roles played by cultural tradition and pragmatism must not be underestimated either.

Ultimately all three of these forces, like the economies of the world themselves, will inevitably interact.

# BIBLIOGRAPHY

For those interested in further comparisons between the various economic systems:

Ebenstein, William. *Today's Isms*. Englewood Cliffs, N.J.: Prentice-Hall, Inc., 1980.
Ellis, Harry B. *Ideals and Ideologies*. New York: World Publishing, 1972.

For those interested in a defense of capitalism:

Friedman, Milton. *Capitalism and Freedom*. Chicago: University of Chicago Press, 1962.

For those interested in the varying faces of Marxist socialism:

Leonhard, Wolfgang. *Three Faces of Marxism*, trans. Ewald Osers. New York: Holt, Rinehart and Winston, 1974.

For readers interested in exploring the economic analyses behind the two great economic systems:

Marx, Karl. *Capital—A Critique of Political Economy*, ed. Frederick Engels, revised and amplified by Ernest Untermann. New York: Modern Library, 1906.

Smith, Adam. *An Inquiry into the Nature and Causes of the Wealth of Nations*, ed., etc. Edwin Cannan, M.A., LL.D. Dunwoody, Georgia: Norman S. Berg, 1976.

# INDEX

Value in use, 18
Value, labor theory of, 46

Wages, 36, 40, 46, 55
Wealth, 9, 53, 54, 58, 77; see
  also Value in exchange;
  Value in use
Wealth of Nations, The. See
  Smith, Adam

Webb, Sydney and Beatrice,
  80
Welfare system, 40
Westward expansion, U.S.,
  59, 65
Whitney, Eli, 30
Women, 33, 38–40
Workers, 35–37, 47, 49; see
  also Labor; Proletariat

# ABOUT THE AUTHOR

Michael Kronenwetter is a free-lance writer who wears many hats. He is a newspaper columnist and media critic, he has written filmstrips, and he has had an award-winning radio play produced by Wisconsin Public Radio.

Mr. Kronenwetter attended Northwestern University and the University of Wisconsin. His books include a history of the region of central Wisconsin where he was raised and now makes his home, and two other books for Franklin Watts: *Are You A Liberal? Are You a Conservative?* and *Free Press v. Fair Trial: Television and Other Media in the Courtroom.*